AFLAME WITHIN

Aflame Within

ALBERT FRANKIE JUNIOR MASELLA

Contents

2018

The Battle Within

Soulmates

Distant Love

Her GoodBye

Without Her

Exposing Reality

Visions Of Her Hazel Eyes

From Ashes To Embers

Our Flame Within

This book is a tribute to my father, as he encouraged me to pursue the woman I loved before he passed away. I wrote every single poem for her, and she would know that when she reads them. I don't need to say her name here because she knows a flame within still carries our love.

~ I ~

2018

YOUR DEVIL

I only danced with your devil
so you don't have to look into his eyes anymore.
I knew the risk, but I believed in us making
it through your past.
That's why regardless if we went our separate ways,
I will not renounce my love for you.
Since our love
hasn't changed if you allowed yourself to see it.
That's because only I can remind you,
only I can love you,
like no other ever could or would dare attempt.

FROM FACELESS TO WANTING LOVE

Seven years ago, my body was a loveless mess.
Until you made a heart once faceless,
open eyes to see the possibilities of love.
With just simple phone calls,
you wouldn't think twice about now.
A story was brewing and yet you lived your life
just like every other day, unaware of that reality.
Confused about the possibility
of us because your heart was faceless.
This drove you into further depression
that came with regrets that
are still effecting you nowadays.
Meanwhile, it drove me into writing a story
I can tell now because you taught me how to love.
Even though it's been a
struggle ever since meeting you.

MY HEART IS UNDER ARREST

You had such an innocent face
to kiss before the waves of different
names took full advantage of those lips.
That made you very hesitant to believe my
lips when you kissed them on the surface.
Even though I would call you gorgeous,
it would go unnoticed because you still felt soulless.
That made everything I did
meaningless when you carried the burden
of your regrets on your sleeves.
That caused your hazel eyes to go blind
from my kindness completely.
That made you unable to see my love,
leaving your heart wide open to be
arrested by the devil.
That's why misery loves your company.

A DREAM WE ONCE SHARED

Are you like everyone else who shares
dreams with their ex after a breakup?
Let me tell you, it's the worst feeling ever.
You can't erase them even if you try
because they always come back unexpectedly.
Only to appear and then disappear without saying a word.
That gives you no time to say what's in your subconscious.
It hurts when they aren't
the person you expected them to be.
It hurts when you realize they
aren't what you pictured them to be.
Yet, the love remains tearing from
the roots of your heart to be free.
However, we keep holding on to it because
it's the key for us to never forget them.
Even though a part of us does,
we can't when the love is truly magical.
It just makes you wonder of what could
have been if circumstances were different.

MY THANK YOU

There isn't one conversation between us I've forgotten.
Each one meant more than the last in taking this broken
man and making him purge himself from his insecurities.
The struggle for me was accepting you were right about
stuff that I was wrong about.
That's where I needed to put my
ego to the side to trust you.
So if you think you were the only one with the
inability to trust, well, you were wrong.
Even though you failed to take my trust entirely
because of your past, I didn't with you.
That ended up being the best decision of my life.
From listening, I learned how much better I can
become, in seeing myself as a real man.
The hazel from your eyes,
showed me my personality
was enticing to show everyone.
That now has crafted a man with
a new perspective on his
life and for that,
I wish I got to thank you.

A REASON NOT GIVEN

How could I forget?
It was just yesterday that I was hearing
your sweet smoothing voice in my ears.
My heart pounding harder the more it
got a taste of your laughter from a distance.
I would climb Mount Everest if that meant
I could be alone in the sound of your voice.
So I can excoriate the clouds with a heart
with our names over the entire earth's surface.
Then you decide to shatter that
possibility with no explanation.
That left my mind heavy with speculation,
causing it to cave in and causing an unstoppable
avalanche of emotions to load my body with anxiety.
For me to ease the jitters, I turned to using
liquor and pills to numb myself.
Regarding why you would break my
heart and ruin our once perfect relationship.

When I lost you,
I lost the only person I ever loved.

~ II ~

THE BATTLE WITHIN

UNSPOKEN WAR

Every day is a battle,
but it's a fight where our hands can't actually help.
Rather, it's our emotions and those aren't
capable of handling this battle like our bones could.
That's why we all handle adversities in different ways
no matter how difficult they may or may not be.
Whether you are housed in
four walls with a dysfunctional family.
If you are dealing with the worries
of adult life regarding your appearance,
or fearing to express your true
self in a judgmental world.
It all doesn't matter
because we are all the same.
Despite even those
who act like they are fine,
they aren't. Instead, their denial makes us
all move backwards and not forward
in expressing ourselves freely.
I'm not one to speak,
I've been the one to act
like I'm fine when I wasn't.
However, it took wanting to be with someone
to take back control of my life.
Which led me to a reality where I could embrace
that purpose without fear of judgment.
So it's time for you to do what I did and that's
discovering your purpose in wanting a better life.
With no need needing to go into war
with yourself anymore.

THE STRUGGLE

Who are you?
Who am I?
To know is to discover.
To discover is to learn.
It doesn't matter if it's family members,
friends or even strangers online
trying to tell us what they believe we want to hear.
However, what they don't realize is that their words
often leave us feeling worse and uncomfortable.
That's because we are deep inside our insecurities.
Hearing new opinions will expose new flaws.
These flaws will cover us up.
However, we reveal our best qualities through the struggle.
If we just acknowledge our imperfections.
That will make us accept the struggle.
Making it possible to be different and that's
ok because that's what makes us special.

CONTROL YOURSELF

Look, you can't escape this hell
when you keep being the animal,
you became on your own.
You can't control yourself and that's
basically why you have no dignity left.
You allow yourself to live in a cage
in your mind and now it's your reality
when you wake up.
We all have a conscious,
yet your behavior says otherwise.
So stop your ways
because not one thing,
an event or state of affairs,
should make you act this way.
You just have to first have the courage
to walk up to the ugly you created.
Look it in the eyes and accept
its hand in understanding with all the bad.
Does indeed come a reason
to save you from yourself.

MY AGONY

It's seven clock, and it's that
time of the day for agony to
relish in my misery
I stand helplessly in the corner,
waiting for it to be over.
That's when I feel abandon
and rather be alone.
I hate it when others try to help,
because realistically I feel like
I deserve this torment.
I cried not from the pain but
from knowing my existence
meant nothing and that if I died,
nobody will care.
That's until you came into my life.
Your support helped me
during the moments in my life I felt lost.
The positivity you brought from your voice
lightened the darkest parts of my mind.
It was because of you.
I could face my agony and banish it
from entering my doors.
I've allowed it to hurt me because
I felt like I deserved it.
Until you showed me no,
I only deserved the best because
I'm an amazing person.

HOW WE REALLY CHANGE

You can stretch your fingers
all you want at the stars,
but that's not how you change your life.
The desire to want more for yourself
comes from being able to turn the
previous page over in your life.
That means stopping the excuses
and being around those that
would enable you into further denial.
You can't use your age as an excuse because
that doesn't define you or
dictate your decision making.
That's why you can't get discouraged
just because you are
older than most when facing the truth.
The most important thing
here is to regain control of your
life and finally free yourself
from its suffocating bitterness.
When in reality it's
what's should have always been
your motivation to better your life.
Instead of trying to reach for God,
and his stars to make a
wish that could never come true.

Life gives you moments to cry about,
only to push you to discover yourself.

~ III ~

SOULMATES

SOULMATES FROM A DISTANCE

I always wanted to escape from my unhappiness.
That was my life.
You always wanted to escape your past mistakes.
That was your life.
However, we both couldn't until fate
led our paths to cross paths
in a world filled with billions.
Little did we know,
God had always planned this because we were
each other's soulmates.
Before he split our
souls apart at birth,
he saw our souls from
a distance able to intertwine.
I realized that to ignite the deepest
love possible between us,
all we needed was to meet.
So when that happened,
we were both able to
fulfill our desires through
countless phone conversations.
This resulted in conversations
that showcased two souls
discovering the truest love imaginable
amongst themselves without even knowing.

NONBELIEVER TO BELIEVE

Before I met you,
I used to chuckle at
the idea that people
could perceive true beauty
as real nowadays
because of the internet.
That's because everyone is obsessed with
plastic surgery and awful looking filters.
These trends have ruined
what we can still call beautiful.
However, it just took you to
stand out from the online crowd
with something others
wish they could buy.
True beauty,
but beauty you can
actually fully grasp
by your eyes being
exactly like a star.
However, according
to God himself,
he crafted the stars
from the very beauty found
in the hazel in your eyes.

YOUR NAME

When I call your name,
it means more than
just getting your attention.
This is how I can satisfy
my dopamine levels so my happiness
can actually take shape.
To create this man with
a legitimate reason to smile.
You can be near me
when I call your name,
or miles away on the phone.
It doesn't matter, the outcome
will be no different because
each piece of you resembles
your beauty to make me whole.
In my eyes, you will see a
longing to keep calling your name,
because I can never get enough of you.
Within my heart, you'll witness the
warmth fill my entire being.
That allows me to come down
from my high peacefully.
Into a sleep, knowing my happiness
and excitement will continue on.
Since all I have to do is mention
your name tomorrow and I
would be whole once again.

YOU MADE ME WHOLE

When you first touch me,
I knew I wanted your body against mine,
because I felt my
soul slipping away.
Your gentle hands could make my
hollow body visible to
feel the sensation of desire.
This made me no longer shy and
just overly excited to be
around you at all times of the day.
You see, it's a known fact that
the day we are born,
our souls do indeed split apart
from us destined to find their
other halves one day.
That was us, and my soul
was aware of it the moment
you touched me.
This connection was undeniable because
I thought I lost everything
before seeing your face.
That's why I couldn't resist
myself from being near you.
So my soul can finally be whole,
and that's why every night,
I looked forward to one thing with you.
That was just always simple
cuddling you in my arms,
so I can feel my soul finally come alive.

I WILL NOT ABANDON OUR LOVE

Instead of being
with you in September,
I was living at a cemetery
where you buried our love.
I wanted to leave, but I couldn't.
As I stood over the grave,
it felt like the love you buried was
reaching out from beneath the earth.
To show me those memories
of us and our phone conversations,
so I wouldn't abandon it.
Especially when you ended it so abruptly,
while it was still vibrant and zesty.
So throughout the night I dug up
our love that was beneath the ground.
Days later, I held our still breathing
love that was covered in your regrets.
That remained enthusiastic
after I removed those
regrets you had done to it.
Since it knew, I will attempt
to rekindle our hearts with its
remains because we were always soulmates.

Your soulmate someday will find you,
because true love will never desert you.

~ IV ~

DISTANT LOVE

A LOVE THEY CANT QUESTION

Enough is enough.
Go tell your parents about me.
About our relationship, about our love.
Since they wouldn't be able to refuse me
because they can't deny our love.
They will understand my love for you because
it's already intensified by the distance.
The burning sensation makes me willing
to go to any lengths to bring
you infinite happiness.
They wouldn't be able to separate us
because our bound is unbreakable.
Even if they tried, it would just
make me more eager to marry you.
Nothing would or could stop me
from seeking everlasting joy with you.

DROWNING IN SORROWS

My love for you clouded the
impending events in our relationship.
You were drowning in your sorrows,
unable to breathe in my love any longer.
All because of what happened in your
last relationship before I joined your life.
Still, I stayed by your side, trying my best
to resuscitate your dying heart
from the overwhelming pain.
I wept in the process because
I was being engulfed in the reality
I was about to lose you.
I remain positive though,
offering you a perspective of us being happy,
as I held your lifeless body in my arms.
However, you couldn't hear my words
any longer because everyone
around you was much louder.
Which affected us, making
you doubt everything about me.
Making you believe I was all a lie and out
to hurt you like everyone else has to you.
Meanwhile, thinking I could handle all of this,
I soon became another casualty in the battle
of loving someone from a distance.
Now I'm left attempting to resolve what's happened
between us because I still hold on to our love.

NOBODY CAN TELL US

Nobody can undermine two individuals
falling in love from a distance.
They can't scoff at the idea that it's impossible
for two people to know if they love each other.
Every single one of us
experiences love uniquely different.
That's what makes the ones
that have a true love so much
more special to read about.
Therefore, anyone who passes judgment
looks ridiculous when finding love is unpredictable.
Love can be just outside or many miles away.
The only way you will know is when you find someone.
Then your heart experiences a burning sensation that
gives you warmth comparable
to a thousand heat waves at once.
Drenching your body in sweat from the countless
butterflies fluttering in your stomach.
That you wouldn't be able to
deny making the love you discover.

STANDING BY LOVE

I will not let you disrespect our love,
regardless if we aren't together.
Your personal issues can not
taint the very essence of our
beauty we once shared.
It's built to handle distance,
every opinion and the unpleasant experiences.
The depth of its affection transcends and
remains beyond anyone's comprehension.
It remains alive,
preserved in a place that nobody can reach.
So here I stand with my hand on my chest,
looking at the miles apart,
remaining sure of one thing.
That I will show what anyone
would if they loved someone,
and that's overcome any
obstacles thrown their way.
While I understand,
these difficulties weren't my fault.
That doesn't mean I will just give up on true love.
All relationships have their
share of uncertainties.
If the love is real, then it
should be prepared to do
what love should do:
step into any difficult situation.
To erase every struggle with relative ease.
Then you will know your love is real like mine.

DISTANCE DOES NOT MATTER WITH YOU

The distance never stopped you
from giving me what any traditional
relationship could give if it was in front of me.
Your personality was a breath of fresh air,
with your intellect, enthusiasm, and sense of humor.
These qualities offer me a greater insight into the
layers I had to peel off my life to grow as a new person.
A voice that would smooth my body with its hands
to feel the sensation of intercourse and love all at once,
making it galvanizing.
This has allowed me to sleep comfortably
as like you were next to me,
because you are always with me
regardless if it was on a phone screen.
Which made seeing your face no different if
it was in person or not because every time was always
more breathtaking than the last.
Any gesture you made had me smiling,
and all your personality quirks made
our conversations memorable.
Your compassion and reliability were
is by the best I have in my life,
because you genuinely were there
when I needed you the most.
That is why their will be no one like you
for me because you are a one of kind,
who is not comparable to anyone else.

It's easy to say I love you and
see those words lose value.

~ V ~

HER GOODBYE

I DON'T WANT TO HURT NO MORE

I don't want to hurt anymore,
but I can't hide from that feeling
because you abandoned me.
You walked away without explanation,
leaving me completely numb.
That has made my mind feel like it
has nothing without you to dream about.
Which has made it collapsed from the thought
I wouldn't be able to see your hazel eyes again.
Incapable of feeling,
as I drown in my tears because my
bathroom is overflowing from the pain.
I can sense a coldness filling the air following
the events that transpired between us.
That's already making me shiver
because my heart feels heavy,
like it has pneumonia.
Despite that, my heart's last words before slipping
into a coma are that I will always love you.
That's what makes your goodbye
a painful reality I now have to live with
because my heart remains yours,
even after your actions that caused me pain.

IN YOUR ABSENCE

I'm stuck in a loop of sadness
because of your absence.
I'm still reaching to
feel your presence.
That getting drunk
is the only way to bring
you back temporarily
for my blood-shot eyes.
The good and bad memories
come and go for me.
However, I will always see the open wound
in my heart left behind from your absence.
A sense of emptiness that
I can't shake off,
no matter how many times I tell myself,
you aren't coming back.
All the while,
a war is going off in my mind.
Where my self inflicted anger is
gunning down every thought of you.
That's when one memory
jumps in front of the gunfire.
To preserve the day,
I told you I love you.

OUR HEARTS APART

You dumped me with no reason given
because you knew one didn't exist.
My kindness was always pure
and the only real cure for your sadness from him.
You carried an incurable virus because of him that
eventually became immune to my temporary cure.
That made you question our love
while you rested your head on your pillow.
That brought our hearts apart,
making you say hurtful things to me
not meant for me, but for him.
The love we once shared was now growing
apart because you thought it was fake.
However, it never broke because it wasn't your fault.
I will never forget when I held you,
with tears in your hazel eyes,
wishing to know when you will be free from him.
That made the reflection in my eyes,
grab your attention because you knew
if he was a cause of us, breaking up.
I will always love you with that same burning sensation,
like if we were back in two thousand eighteen again.

TIME HEALS ALL

The more time has withered away.
I understand loving you as fiercely
as I did was like wielding
a double-edged sword.
I believed you would
return my love with kindness.
Not struggle externally with it.
Trust with you was such a fragile thing,
something I didn't fully grasp.
Now I do, but I have no regrets about
giving you all my love right away.
Even if that meant
I got hurt unintentionally
by you because of your
inability to trust my feelings.
The time we shared in the summer
was so worth your painful goodbye.
Our love was so undeniable that it
forced us to see each other at the
worst possible time for either of us.
Totally worth it,
because it's what we needed.
When you put aside all that
sadness from us breaking up.
You would see nowadays a changed man,
both in appearance and mindset.
It took being with you to understand true love.
It took losing you to be inspired
to go rediscover it once again.

OUR LAST NIGHT IS OUR NEW BEGINNINGS

I saw it in your eyes,
and that's all I wanted all my life.
To say I love you,
without saying
the words because of my heart
already knew them.
You are who I've been
looking for, and yet here I stand,
remembering my last time I hugged you.
That was the last time I was actually happy,
before eventually you made your
goodbye my reality with your last words.
Those words hurt so much,
because they told the story
that I would inevitably
damage my deepest desire,
which was to love you.
The only thing I ever wanted
since two thousand eighteen.
Although your entire life has
been awful and your
relationship was no different.
Our relationship wasn't,
because it was our phone conversations
that made you forget about him.
It was I who opened your wings
to help you fly away from him,
just like you open my wings to
regain my confidence back.
Our relationship may have ended,

but that's just fate guiding us onto
different paths for a specific purpose.
So the next time we meet,
we will rekindle this love because
we will finally have learned to love
ourselves to make that our reality.

Your goodbye could either be a painful reminder
or a reason to become better.

~ VI ~

WITHOUT HER

YOU ARE GONE

Today is just like yesterday,
because it's all the same when
you are no longer a part of them.
The struggle to keep my faith seems
unfeasible when it was fate
that brought us together.
Meanwhile, I continue to watch
the layers of our love,
we built that extend deeper than the Mariana Trench
disintegrating into nothing.
That's because my love for you is under attack
with the inner struggle
of me trying to keep you,
but I'm losing the battle.
Thus resulting in me becoming
comatose because I just overdose
with an endless cycle of losing you.
That's what came from loving you,
because that meant accepting the devil
into our bed because he was your past.
That I completely ignored because
I was ignorant in believing we can
make it work when you couldn't even love yourself.

COLORLESS

Paint will dip off walls that aren't clean.
The same applies to trying to love someone.
If the surface isn't ready, it will struggle to stick.
Mixing colors doesn't work at all.
Thickening the coat can't hide the cracks behind the layers.
Chucks peel because it's human nature to continue to try,
but some are just meant to be colorless forever.
That's something you will just have to accept,
like I sadly did.

A FRACTURE I APPRECIATED

To wish is to dream of a different timeline accordingly.
I don't because the love we made
brought me here in this universe.
Even though if it was difficult,
to see the one thing I truly love hurt me.
When your stupidity and ignorance were on full display.
However, unintentionally,
your actions healed my inability to walk.
Now I stand, not wanting to fight the love we made.
Rather instead remembering
I couldn't have experienced it without you.

A HEART I SHALL RECLAIM

The day you told me you loved me,
you invited me into your heart.
When you gave me the keys and kissed me goodbye,
I felt nothing but joy.
Excitement coursing through my body,
knowing I'm going to spend the rest of my life with you.
However, as I made myself at home,
I noticed the four walls of your heart being
consumed by uncertainties.
All happening because of years
of you being mistreated by others.
The air in your heart evaporated soon after
because you wanted me out.
That's when I had to make
the toughest decision of my entire life.
Stay trying to improve our situation
when that was impossible or die trying.
I left because I knew you better than anyone else could.
That's why,
unlike the others, that hurt you.
You gave me all
the keys to your heart.
Since you knew if this happens,
I could one day return them back
and turn on the engine to start your heart
into accepting my love once again.

THE NIGHT I TOOK YOUR DEVIL

On our last day together,
I couldn't bring myself to say I love you.
This was because I felt lifeless,
as if I was already dead and prepared
to be placed in the body bag crafted by your past.
Since it knew you would shout
those words from your mouth at me,
striking me dead like bullets to the heart.
This all beginning because of him,
which led you to compare me to
him to feel what you kept seeing.
Now, without you,
I'm left with the devil I accepted into my life.
That came from loving someone like you,
but I sacrificed to be with you.
Regardless if your past was
full of sins and regrets.
However, your devil can't
control me like he could with you.
That's because he can't possess
a soul that's now an angel.

When you cry about the past,
you'll let go of what doesn't last.

~ VII ~

EXPOSING REALITY

EXPOSING YOUR DEVIL

I already knew before I told you I loved you,
that I could lose you any second
because of your life being unstable.
For that, I didn't need to search for
reasons we weren't together.
I had no chance of coming this early
to face the devil living in your mind.
Ready to threaten me by turning you against me if
I dared show you genuine love.
Intentionally sabotaging our relationship
by making your life crumble before our eyes.
I couldn't stop that avalanche
of doubt from coming down.
Designed to swallow me up and bury me alive.
However, that's in the past now, and I currently have
your devil trapped in my mind.
To be behind my eyes to see me
motivated to fix the heartbreak
that came along with loving you.

EXPOSING A NIGHTMARE

You cannot expose a nightmare.
That is because it exposes your fears first
before you have time to confront it in your sleep.
I'm sure you feel your chest tightening
every night with that undeniable regret.
That it is always burning
hotter than any sun imaginable.
We all do indeed deserve that
closure from heartbreak.
However, in today's society,
nobody has sympathy.
Society has raised people
with zero empathy.
That's what makes it amusing
when people preach
religious morals when they
are just all demons in disguise.
Always ready to use and abuse the
innocent because they have no soul.
The devil already claimed their soul at birth.
In exchange for hurting, individuals like you and me.

EXPOSING YOU

If you come from a troubled past,
you can't love another just yet.
Otherwise, you will purposely
project your heartbreak onto them.
Then start blaming them for pouring a
bottle of salt onto your wounded heart;
when all they wanted to do was just
help you because they love you.
However, having a dysfunctional mind
prevents you from functioning effectively.
It causes you to be more increasingly distant.
That if your partner attempts to bridge the gap.
They will only end up receiving
the backlash of your venom.
So I suggest you learn from my experience,
and not love another if you can't love yourself.
Otherwise, you will cause long-term damage
to someone's ability to trust another again.

THE TRUTH BEHIND THIS HEARTBREAK

You can drink all you want,
but you won't deceive yourself
about your current situation.
You can avoid confrontation all you want,
but you wouldn't be able to
get rid of the issue at hand.
Each wine bottle just holds a
reflection of a person who's a failure.
You can convince others you are fine behind
your ugly photos that you put a smile on.
However, I got to see you beneath your mask.
You can't outrun your past
because it will always catch you.
The terrible decisions you made
are everlasting in your existence.
Along with every degrading act
you put your body through.
Your mistakes come with consequences,
just as heartbreak inevitably
came by loving someone like you.
You could avoid the truth for as long as you like,
but you wouldn't outlast your reality.

Blame your faults on others.
You'll end up making new ones.

~ VIII ~

VISIONS OF HER HAZEL EYES

MY PARADISE

A world without you in it
is a world that can't be another heaven.
A place isn't a place worth remembering
if you aren't a part of the memory.
Anyone would say, "I'm very fortunate to have
the luxury to take vacations and
go anywhere I want at any time."
However, I say, "not really, because for
me to actually get a true slice of paradise,
takes you coming through my front doors right now."
That's all because of your lovely face that holds the hazel
between your eyes that makes me
want to melt into my bed.
To wait for your warmth to warm
our covers under the blankets.
That gives me my personal heaven,
ignoring God all together.
Since when my bed has you in it,
that's truly heaven and one the
Gods above can never match even if they tried.

YOUR VOICE IS MY ADDICTION

Your personality is sweet
like a bowl of sugar and that's why
you are my Sweet Cheeks.
When I hear you talk, I just want to pour
every delightful word that escapes your lips across mine.
That is how I can get my heartstrings
to tug a harpsichord melody.
So the sweet sound of your voice can sugar
my veins with your love that's intoxicating.
The tone is scorching hot, but that allows me
to savor the sweetness of your every word.
That has me hooked and driven for more of you.
So don't get upset when I can't put down
the telephone even though you are tired.
My ears just crave the exquisite beauty
that emanates from your vocal cords.
To provide them with the sweetness of your voice
for them to get the message over to my mind to go to sleep.

A BEAUTY LIKE NO OTHER

You walked into beauty at birth,
because the moment you were born,
true beauty entered the world.
That's why no amounts of money
could ever buy the beauty you possess.
You were a butterfly shedding from it's cocoon
gradually instead of forcibly like others.
To show your wings doesn't need artificial enhancements
unlike so many that attempt to fly like you.
You lead the path for what's it is like to be
the golden standard for every woman.
That all wishes they have the natural beauty
you have with no surgery or make up.
Beauty that doesn't need photo filters or fillers.
A face that makes you understand right away
how amazing the sight of you truly is to their eyes.

READY TO ARGUE

I've been waiting patiently
to discuss this topic with you.
That's about your thinking
you are just only beautiful,
with nothing else to offer.
Whether your insecurities come out,
I frankly don't care.
You see, you can swirl up a range of feelings within
one's heart by simply a touch or a blank stare.
To ignite a storm of feelings
that go straight to the mind.
For their previous thoughts to become relevant
to their understanding of time.
Every woman dreams of recreating that
but can't because they aren't you.
Unlike others,
your best attributes go beyond
just your physical appearance.
You encapsulate beauty into wanting to
fall in love when anyone gets to know you.

YOUR BEAUTY MEANT EVERYTHING

It took me losing you,
for me to discover how lost I was
without your hazel eyes in my dreams.
Your eyes drove my thoughts to write
material throughout the night to comfort
those that could never feel happiness.
They were an arch of colors formed by your
genetics at birth that brought true beauty into this world.
Every morning, I would wake up excited,
knowing I dreamt of you because
that meant I get to pen down
more ways to describe your beauty to others.
It's true drugs could stimulate
one's dopamine levels,
but when they receive a dose,
of your beauty through my words,
you completely had the power to cure them.
You may have not believed or understood me,
however, as I've said,
"You meant more to me than you would ever imagine."
You were really my purpose
to take your beauty
you held and make it into pure
encouragement through my words.

MISSING YOU

Although we never had a chance together
because every other guy
you dated hurt you.
It was always us before them,
I will always say to you.
This means I will love you forever,
despite losing you.
My home will never be the same
without you
because you are nowhere
to be found.
Although I could pretend
you were all a dream,
my heart could never
do such a thing.
I look at the couch,
 feeling my heart
sink to the bottom,
knowing that's where you once sat.
The lasting memory of your
hazel eyes reminding me.
That nothing in this entire universe
could ever compare to your beauty.
Since looking at you created everlasting joy
that makes you paint my heart a bright red.
All because only you
could make me blush
from heart to cheek with your hazel eyes.

YOUR HAZEL EYES

Your hazel eyes glow with a hue
reminiscent of the radiant
light from rainbows filtering
through the earth's atmosphere.
This dazzling effect transforms
the world into a display of green gems
shining in place of stars—much like an angel
unfolding its wings for the very first time.
When any light hits the hazel in your iris,
it crystallizes like a glacier splitting from the snow.
This reveals a lighter greenish tint that
highlights the brilliance of your eyes.
That keeps its radiance
glowing to provide
a warmth akin to the sun's most intense
rays one could ever fathom.
That's why my heart is always
ready to connect with you, whether
it's face to face or on my phone.
Since only you can provide this type of
excitement to pulse through my veins.
To make it flow
through my bloodstream,
to deliver that exhilarating rush
of dopamine.

Your beauty transcends through
the laws of the universe.

~ IX ~

FROM ASHES TO EMBERS

A HAZEL WITHIN ME

I can't lie, but all my pictures of you
are fading nowadays into black and white.
Memories, once vibrant, now clinging
on to the beauty of your hazel eyes.
In hopes it might just be the cure
for my emotional blindness.
I feel utterly drained,
unable to perceive life
as I did when you were with me.
When you left me,
you took away your hazel eyes.
That was my comfort of seeing beauty
as I come to know it in this world.
So now that your hazel has closed its eyelids on me,
it feels like the sun has set upon me.
To be left in the darkness, but a flame
remains within these photos of you.
That makes me no longer emotionally blind,
but emotionally ready to go see your hazel eyes
once again through the fire of your devil.

I CAN'T FORGET HER

When you love someone,
it's difficult for anyone else to comprehend
that because they don't know your feelings.
They can't feel what you feel,
they can just hear what you tell them.
That makes them form an opinion
that's pretty much worthless.
That's why others don't get why
I feel so strongly about her;
feeling love doesn't mean you
truly will understand it.
Love will reveal itself as one
of two types of ashes arising
from the burnt sensation in the aftermath.
My ashes showed purity and brightness
because I stumbled upon love.
That's why I would never forget about her.

OUR WHITE ASHES

I shall keep thy ashes of this ember warm
by cradling it in my hands and
throwing it into the sky with anger.
That will allow the remaining remnants
that are white to become a cascade
of color to bleed through the night.
A color that is your favorite,
and despite your devil's best efforts,
he wouldn't be able to stop this newly crafted gemstone
from forming in the fire.
This fire burns a love that's a bluish color
to represent the difficulties of losing you
and that cause me to lose my life.
Meanwhile, the ashes now are a gemstone
that's holds a reflection in its glass shape body
of us throughout the years.
All our messages to phone conversations that lasted hours.
To us finally meeting and for that I grip it
because now it carries our love.
For me to rest it on my chest
for my heart to know it's finally over for me to stop hurting
knowing you aren't coming back and that's perfectly ok.

MY FIRST WORDS

I may not be the richest man
alive on this planet.
The world may be full of
millionaires and billionaires,
thinking they have it all.
They may believe they have
everything that anyone in this world
or could ever desire materialistic wise.
However, they would be all wrong
because they don't have the most valuable
possession in our existence
and that is your love to feel.
I knew this the moment
I first spoke to you many years ago
because I saw the type of person
you truly were in real time.
That's when eventually
you told me your past scars, and I didn't
blink at anything you were saying because
I could had care less about any of your insecurities.
I stare deeply into your eyes next to let you know
any imperfections you had in your
thoughts or on your skin meant
absolutely nothing to me.

This also including any past mistakes you may have made,
because my first words I said many years ago to you
can't be altered because I meant them.
Those words were if you forgot,

"I see tremendous beauty radiating from
within you because your hazel eyes
shine as bright as the stars of the night."

True love is always one phone call away,
because it's always on time when you need it the most.

~ X ~

OUR FLAME WITHIN

YOU ARE THE FIRST

You are the first to not just make me want a relationship.
However, make me want one to take it seriously that
I would want marriage and to start a family with you.
Whatever that may look like, if that's with our
biological children, adoption, or is just having cats.
It doesn't matter either way because just the
thought of us together with our
new family brings undeniable joy.
Home is where the heart says love is
and that's with you I've learned.
The more I'm with you, the more
I felt the sweet relief of my issues
at work, bills, and stress go away.
That's because I know
coming home to you
will make me forget and
remember why you were the first.

I LOVE YOU

Amidst the city lights,
I've always picture us sitting holding hands.
Both of our hearts glowing red because of
our flame within that's still burning.
That is painting every night we are
together with our kisses that are illuminating
love among the stars.
That the city has taken notice and
has put the spotlight on us to feel
the affection from above.
Making me take you, so we can go running,
intertwining our fingers
together on the way;
to painting the walls of this world red.
So I can confess my love for you
to everyone to know, by my fingers
being covered in paint from
my love I've wrote on the city's walls.

THE QUESTION

Ever since I knew I loved you,
I've struggled to ask this one question.
I've discussed this countless times with
families and friends for their opinion.
Every answer taken into consideration
and put next to the vows I wrote for you back
in two thousand eighteen.
It is true you can't hold on to every memory,
but with you,
you are the exception to the rule.
That's because we commemorate
this love through heartbreak,
so when we close our eyes,
we know we will have each other.
To forever appreciate this love because
even through the hardest times
we had recently,
my question hasn't changed since last that
I wanted to ask you.
That's always simply been me asking you,
"Would you marry me?"

THE VOWS I WROTE

At the end of two thousand eighteen,
I wrote this because this is how I envision
the day I would propose to you.
When the day comes when I get
on one knee, the atmosphere
will glimmer bright white like a snowy
blanket that's hovering over us, created
by the heavens for this special evening.
That every snowflake that
falls sparkles a light to give
us a clear path to move forward.
The candles I set will flicker,
but the wax will never melt
because it's been burning
for years for this moment to happen.
Our footsteps will glow from
behind in the snow amidst the
love we have built from afar.
As you look away at the chilly
atmosphere, admiring the scenery.
I will hug you from behind and turn
you around to kiss you. To look you in
the eyes, and tell you, "I love you."
As I get on one knee to ask you,
"Will you marry me?" Now we enter
two thousand nineteen, and that's when
I wrote these vows for you. They said,
"I discovered my love for you in two thousand eighteen.
You inspired me; you motivated me and honestly made my
dreams of ever finding love come true.

Every second with you is a feeling of a celebration,
as if you are every wonderful holiday put together.
It's just like how my dad always envisioned
for me when I was growing up.
He told me I would find that special someone,
and when I opened my heart to you completely,
I knew immediately that you were the one.
Now Valentine's Day is no longer a holiday for me
because every day with you is my Valentine's Day."

AFLAME MY DAD SAW IN US

When I was a little boy many years ago,
I would be always outside running around with my soccer ball.
I was so innocent, yet so clueless to the evils in this world.
That's when I became a victim, and just another voice
that went unheard, which made it difficult for me to open up.
Twenty-eight years later and the evening came when
my father passed away, the only family I had left.
I still remember it like yesterday because I wouldn't
have pursue you without his blessing.
So here is our last conversation:
"Do you remember what I told
you when you were younger?"
I responded, "Of course I do, Dad."
He then said, "It's time to go after her now.
She's been waiting long enough to feel
the love you have within yourself for her."
My father's voice weaken by the bloody coughs,
as he reached for my hand to convey his message;
"Son... prove to her you love her like you
showed me all these years you talked about her."
That was the last breath he took before slipping
into a deep sleep to never awake again;
tears welled up as I clutched his
hand and promised softly; "I will Dad."
When I bravely revealed my feelings to you,
it was me allowing you into my innocent
heart that was hurt as a child.
So when you took my heart,
you made a scared hurt boy
into a confident man,

full of everlasting love,
like my dad always wanted because he knew
the only way I could heal
was by your love.
That he was right about,
and for that I thank you
for this a flame within.

I don't need a ring to tell me we are together,
you will know the moment I tell you I love you.